CONTENTS

PLATO

FOR BEGINNERS

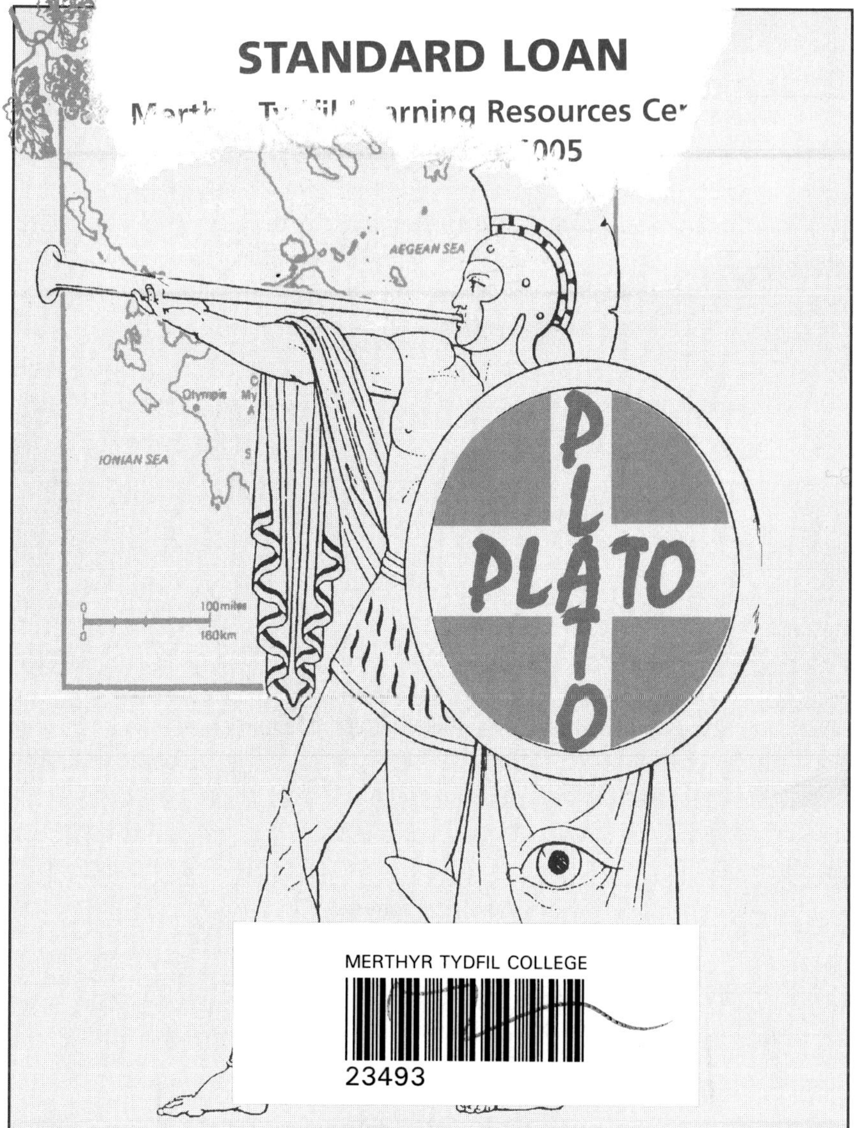

AEGEAN SEA

Olympia

IONIAN SEA

0   100 miles

0   160km

PLATO

PLATO

ROBERT CAVALIER

ILLUSTRATIONS BY ERIC LURIO

For Beginners LLC
62 East Starrs Plain Road
Danbury, CT 06810 USA
www.forbeginnersbooks.com

A For Beginners® Documentary Comic Book
Originally published by Writers and Readers, Inc.
Copyright © 1997, 1998

Cataloging-in-publication information is available from the Library of Congress.

ISBN-10 # 1-934389-08-0 Trade
ISBN-13 # 978-1-934389-08-9 Trade

Manufactured in the United States of America

For Beginners® and Beginners Documentary Comic Books® are published
by For Beginners LLC.

Reprint Edition

WHO WAS PLATO?

First of all, Plato was not a god or a superman.
—He was a man. —All men are mortal. —Therefore,
Plato was a mortal. Flesh and blood, and let's not
forget it!

More specifically, Plato was a philosopher —
perhaps the greatest the world has ever known.

But what is a philosopher?

—Someone who deals with philosophy (a Greek word meaning "love of wisdom"). So why should we care about wisdom? In answer to that question, Aristotle, a student of Plato, once said:

"The wise man is to the ignorant as the living is to the dead."

What Does that Mean?

It means that understanding the world, ourselves, and how we know what we know...makes our lives deeper, more meaningful — basically, BETTER!

Besides, as a species we seem to have a need to ask...

Plato's approach to this question — and the answers he arrived at — changed the way we think about the world and our place within it.

Plato's influence has been so great that a prominent modern philosopher, ALFRED NORTH WHITEHEAD, once declared:

"The safest general characterization of the whole Western philosophical tradition is that it consists of a series of footnotes to Plato."

Alfred North Whitehead

Plato was the first to write about many of the things we today take for granted:

What is truth?
Justice?
Beauty?

(And asking "What's it all about?" was part of the Greek way.)

Plato's answers to these and many other questions had a profound effect on the future of:

Religion

Economics

Art

Psychology

History

Science

MATH

POLITICS

Literature

Love

EVERYTHING!!!

OUR STORY BEGINS LONG, LONG AGO IN A CIVILIZATION FAR, FAR AWAY...

Today, we tend to think of Greek art and culture as "Classical." By that we mean cool, clean lines, white marble sculpture, tapering columns — grace and restraint. **In reality, Greek buildings and statues were painted in bright, garish colors.**

The paint wore off over time, thus leaving us with the wrong impression. The Greeks, as we know from their writing, were actually a people torn between reason and madness, freedom and slavery, war and peace, life and death.

In the year 428 B.C., Plato was born into this world — the center of which was the important city-state ("polis") of Athens. High above the walls encircling the city was the Acropolis — the temples built to honor the gods. Foremost of all was the goddess Athena, protectress of the city. The embodiment of strength in peace, Athena ruled over this cradle of philosophy.

Athens was one of the oldest city-states in Greece. Its foundation is lost in the mists of pre-history. But by Plato's time, it had grown into the richest, most populous Greek city. Its central location and access to the sea made it the commercial and cultural center of Hellas, the Greek world.

Greece was poor in natural resources. It was dry, with few rivers. The soil was great for growing olives and grapes, but other crops grew with difficulty. The land was cut up by mountain ranges and divided by water, especially the Peloponese and the islands of the Aegean.

This physical situation encouraged the growth of small self-sufficient city-states. All shared a common language and basic culture, but sometimes little else. In fact, the Greeks seemed to enjoy fighting each other more than anyone else.

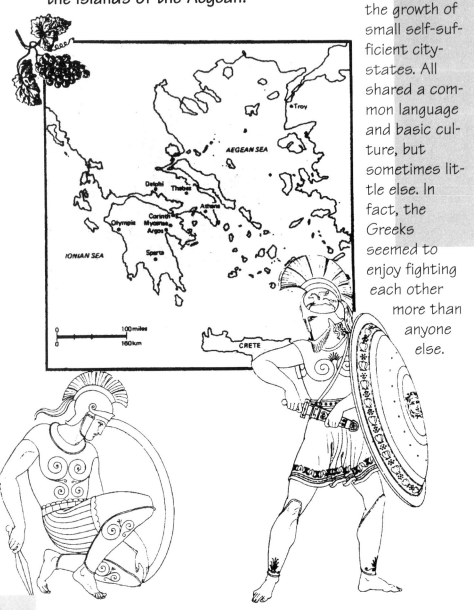

Politically, Greek city-states were organized in one of three ways:

AUTOCRACY— rule by one, king or tyrant

OLIGARCHY— rule by the few, the noble and the rich

DEMOCRACY— rule by the many, or the people as a whole

> Athens was known as the birthplace of democracy.
> In reality, it was a three-tiered society.

THE FIRST TIER consisted of all the male citizens, ranging from wealthy landowners to merchants and even including poor laborers.

THE SECOND TIER consisted of free women and resident foreigners.

THE THIRD TIER consisted of the large slave population.

Only the male citizens could vote in the Assembly and hold positions in the Council, which governed the city-state.

The political evolution of Athens went through many stages. At first, it was a primitive monarchy led by hereditary kings. Then, the land-owning aristocrats assumed control. The earliest experiments in democracy were the reforms of Solon, which failed because of imbalances of power and clan rivalries. They were followed by an oligarchy in which power was based on wealth. **Tyrants, whose authority was based on military force, eventually seized power. They were able to rule by playing the poor against the rich.**

Finally, in 510 B.C., the last tyrant, Hippias, was banished. Democracy was re-established on a sounder footing when Cleisthenes, a popular leader, called the people into a reorganized assembly.

Athenian democracy got its first real test during the Persian Wars (ca. 500-450 B.C.). In the year 480 B.C., Xerxes, the Persian king, actually succeeded in burning Athens. But the valor of the Athenian navy — manned by free citizens — destroyed the Persian forces at the battle of Salamis.

The victory gave Athens a new importance in the region, based on its sea power — and it gave the Athenian citizenry a new political importance, since aristocratic domination of the old land-based, cavalry-led army was no longer the military bulwark of the state.

After the war, the city was rebuilt under Pericles. **But this took money**. The Athenians raised the necessary funds in an age-old way ....

WE STOLE THEM!

Former allies were squeezed dry. The common treasury on the holy island of Delos was looted. What had been a defensive federation of the Greeks quickly became an Athenian empire.

Then, for what may have seemed like no reason at all, a small squabble between two Greek towns erupted into a major power confrontation between Athens and her arch-rival Sparta.

Athens' former colonies quickly defected. Spartan troops marched north and actually camped just outside the city. The Athenians, for their part, were content to sit behind their protective walls and fight by sea.

Then disaster struck in the form of...

PLAGUE

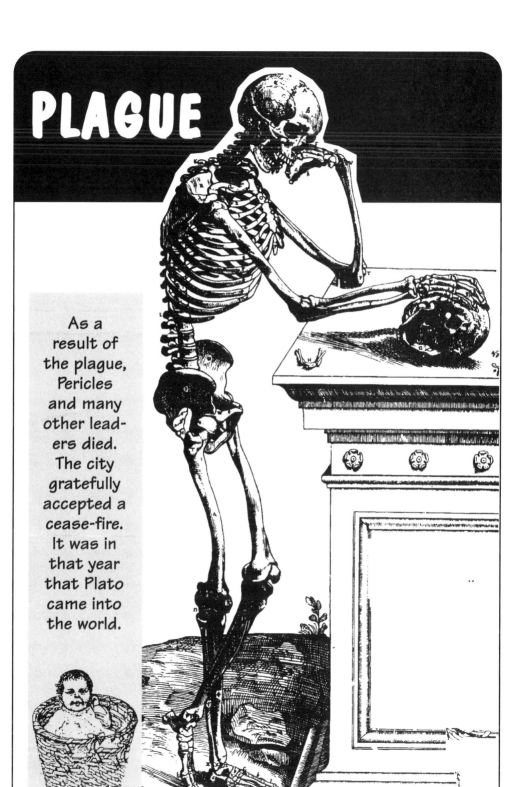

As a result of the plague, Pericles and many other leaders died. The city gratefully accepted a cease-fire. It was in that year that Plato came into the world.

Plato was born into one of Athens' oldest and most aristocratic families. Boys of his class were generally educated at home by tutors. Their studies included learning to write on tablets, reading the books of Homer, and playing music.

Other lessons were taught in the gymnasium. Here a boy learned to develop his body through exercise and sport. Not only would this training build character, but it would also prepare young men for military service in defense of their city-state.

Young Plato probably got a different kind of education on his walks through the Agora, the open marketplace of Athens. For here he may have heard the strange-sounding words of a certain truth-seeker who couldn't help but cause trouble wherever he went:

THE LIFE OF SOCRATES

Who was Socrates? We know that he was born sometime in the year 469 or 470 B.C., and that he might have been the son of a midwife and a laborer. He claimed at one-time that he could trace his ancestry back to the mythic sculptor Dædalus.

> Is there any reason why lovers of the truth can't cause a little trouble now and then?

We also know that **Socrates never wrote down a word of philosophy in his life**. What we know of his character and his thought comes from the writing of two of his students — Plato and Xenophon. Both men wrote their accounts years after the death of their mentor. Yet there can be no doubt that Socrates, more than any other man who ever lived, changed the face of philosophy forever.

> And he also has to receive high marks for being one of the greatest troublemakers and busybodies in all recorded history.

It's only human nature to wonder about our origins and our place in the universe. In ancient civilizations the answer to this question had always turned around religion and fate. Gods and goddesses were responsible for the creation of the universe and often took a hand in the lives of mortals.

But in the Greek world, people began to wonder if forces other than the mysterious gods has a role in the universe. Various thinkers tried to understand the universe in purely material terms. They were called the PHYSICALISTS. In many ways they were the forerunners of today's scientists.

The Physicalist philosophers soon focused on the Elements.

- Some claimed that all things were made of **Earth**.

- Others insisted it was *Air*.

- And still others argued for **FIRE** or *Water*.

An important philosopher named Demosthenes simplified things. Everything, he declared, was made from tiny bits of indestructible matter bumping into each other and sticking together. He called these invisible particles "atoms."

As for Socrates, he seems to have been born curious. As a youth, he was attracted to the ideas of the Physicalists. But eventually he turned his attention away from natural science toward the problems of everyday life. Here he encountered the **Sophists**. These were relativists and skeptics who claimed that the only important thing in life was to get what you want — and the only way to get it was to persuade others to give it to you.

They specialized in the art of **rhetoric**, since it is primarily through speaking well that you persuade others to agree with your opinion.

As Protagoris said:

"Man is the measure of all things."

Might is Right

But Socrates was deeply disturbed by these "practical responses" to human conduct. He saw immediately that if there is no "**truth**," and if there is only "**opinion**" and the ability to persuade the others, then what would stop one from arguing that there is no "justice" or — worse yet — that "justice" is simply the advantage of the stronger? (Might is right.) And what would be the consequences of that position on a society that held it? (Athens was already bullying its "allies" into giving more tribute.)

He also saw the absurdity of a position that argued that judgments about right and wrong are relative to the individual.

When a person is ill, do you hold the physician's opinion on par with the carpenter's; and when a house is to be built, do you go to a physician or to a carpenter? It seems that we DO recognize that some people have a knowledge in these matters and others don't. Why not also in moral and political matters?

Socrates believed that a knowledge of goodness, justice, beauty, and so forth was indeed possible. **In fact, such a knowledge was necessary before we act** (we should **KNOW** justice before we practice politics).

Beyond this, Socrates held the view that if we did KNOW what, for instance, "justice" really is, then we would actually BE just. People only do wrong things because they are ignorant of what the right thing really is! (One would never choose the lesser over the better.)

So it became of the utmost importance for Socrates to discover what the good life really was. He was not concerned with the nature of the universe (like the Physicalists), and he was not concerned with merely winning the argument (like the Sophists). Rather, he was concerned with human matters and with finding out the truth of those matters.

But how to carry out this search?

The Good Life

One day, around 460 B.C., the great philosopher Parmenides came to town accompanied by his pupil Zeno. Pamenides impressed Socrates with the idea of Permanence. <u>Reality, Parmenides argued, is Unchanging</u>.
Zeno supported his mentor's position by reducing to absurdity any assertion that motion and change really do exist.

CONSEQUENCES

ACT

Socrates took this method of refutation and used it in his quest for the truth. An example of it is found in Plato's Gorgias: If you say that Goodness and Pleasure are the same, then is the person who is enjoying scratching his head also a person who is living the good life? And what of "bad pleasures" (like the tyrant who enjoys killing)? If the action gives him pleasure, is it therefore good?

To this method of refutation Socrates added a search for definition.

An example of this is found in Plato's Euthyphro:

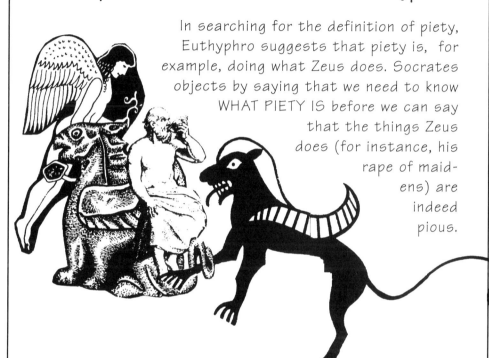

In searching for the definition of piety, Euthyphro suggests that piety is, for example, doing what Zeus does. Socrates objects by saying that we need to know WHAT PIETY IS before we can say that the things Zeus does (for instance, his rape of maidens) are indeed pious.

Socrates developed a passion for this stuff. He'd carry on a conversation with anyone and everyone. But this is not the only unique aspect of Socrates' life...

Socrates' style and character made him one of the most interesting men in town. Short and stout, with bulging eyes and a pug nose, he made quite a sight. We hear of him "staring with wide open eyes, as his custom was," "glancing up with head lowered like a bull," and "casting his eyes sidelong."

He could not only out talk and out think everyone, he could also out fight and out drink them as well.

Socrates attracted the aristocratic youth of Athens (Plato's uncle, **Critias**, was among the followers). It was great fun to watch Socrates in action.

Pompous people were often put in their place by Socrates' relentless questioning. And kids could go home and try out some of these "Socratic" arguments on their bewildered parents.

Socrates quickly became the hit of the agora. All sorts of people flocked to hear him.

Word had it that his daimon, or protecting spirit, specifically prevented him from doing or saying anything wrong.

YOU JUST LOVE ME FOR MY MIND!

One day a sickly friend of Socrates', named Chairephon, made a journey to the Delphic Oracle — one of the most sacred temples in all of Greece. After being purified, he asked the priests to deliver to the Oracle the question: **"Who was the wisest of all mortals?"** The Oracle went into a trance and, speaking for the god Apollo, proclaimed:

"No one is wiser than Socrates."

Shocked and confused by the saying (he thought himself "most ignorant"), Socrates made a determined effort to find someone wiser than himself.

Although he had no trouble finding people who claimed to be wise, none could actually prove their wisdom under questioning.

It began to dawn on Socrates— **"I am wiser than they in this small respect: that I know that I do not know, whereas they think they know something when they really don't."**

The solution to the riddle of the Oracle is found in the dual notion of <u>Socratic Ignorance</u> and <u>Socratic Wisdom</u>.

The Ignorance is a not-knowing in the sphere of values (justice, goodness, etc.).
The Wisdom is an awareness of the ignorance.
What separated Socrates from all the others was simply the fact the he was aware of his ignorance, while they were ignorant of their ignorance. In this respect, Socrates was the "wisest" among them all.

But throughout all this, the Peloponnesian War raged on — and Socrates was in the thick of it...

In 424 B.C., Socrates, fighting as a foot soldier, showed great courage during the Athenian defeat at Delium.

That same year "Socrates" appeared as the lead character in Aristophanes' new comedy — The Clouds.

Despite the comedy at home, the defeat at Delium had a sobering effect. The internal politics of Athens were divided among those who wanted to continue the fighting and those who now wanted peace.

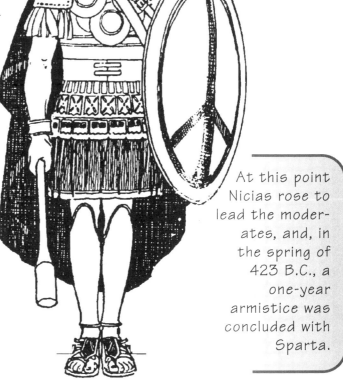

At this point Nicias rose to lead the moderates, and, in the spring of 423 B.C., a one-year armistice was concluded with Sparta.

Cleon, a demagogue who had taken control after the death of Pericles, led a force north to Amphipolis (422 B.C.).

There he met his death. The death of Cleon resulted In a victory for the forces of peace. In 421 B.C., Athens and Sparta concluded the "Peace of Nicias."

Plato, by this time, was beginning his education. (We can imagine Plato questioning Homer's Illiad and Odyssey: Was it right for the gods to lie and rape, as Homer said they did?)

During the "Peace of Nicias," Athens turned her attention to tightening control of her empire. Any rebellion was harshly dealt with. For example, in the "dialogue with Melos," the generals argued that because they were stronger, they were right.

In 415 B.C., Athens saw an opportunity to expand its empire to include the Italian city of Syracuse.

A great expedition was formed under the leadership of Nicias and Alcibiades.

Shortly before the departure of the invading force, a sacrilege was committed (the destruction of several hermes — sacred roadside markers). When the ships had already set sail, people began to suspect that Alcibaides, in a drunken revelry, had made fun of the mystery religions and had been responsible for the broken hermes. He was recalled from the expedition, but he fled instead to Sparta (where he was welcomed until he seduced the king's wife).

The expedition continued without him... .

ADVANCE TO THE FRONT!

THINGS DID NOT BODE WELL FOR THE ATHENIANS.

Syracuse proved stronger than thought — and eventually Sparta (with Alcibiades' advice) became involved. By 413 B.C., Nicias was about to retreat when an eclipse of the moon made him think otherwise. His superstition proved fatal — the Athenians were defeated (they lost over 200 ships and 10,000 men). No one returned from the expedition — the Athenians only heard of the defeat through a conversation someone had while getting a haircut.

The defeat emboldened the colonies to revolt and Sparta to resume hostilities.

Sparta held a fort just outside Athens (Plato was now in the cavalry and was probably harassing the Spartan forces there). The instability at this time made it possible for the conservative oligarchs to rise to power. Once in power (411 B.C.), they became known as the Four Hundred. They were soon overthrown, however, when a collaboration with the Spartans was uncovered. In that same year democracy was restored.

But the restored democracy swung to the most drastic extremes of political passion.

A demagogue, Cleophon, roused the people in the false hope that Athens could once again regain its greatness. Revenge against political opponents and the old hatred of Sparta were stirred up.

In 406 B.C., however, Athens suffered a serious setback at Notium. In the winter of that year, the Athenian fleet gained a hard-won victory near Mytilene. However, severe winds and possibly negligent leadership prevented the rescue of many Athenian sailors from the wreckage.

When news of this reached Athens, a great public outcry demanded that the generals be tried and executed as a group.

It so happened that on that day Socrates was in charge of the Council, which essentially governed the city.

In preparing the business for the Assembly, he refused to go against the Athenian law that forbade mass trials. He bravely stood up against the mob in the Council of 500.

However, he was outmaneuvered, and the generals were soon tried and executed.

THE WAR CONTINUED...

In 405 B.C., **most of Athens' remaining** soldiers found themselves and **their fleet in the north near** the Hellespont.

It was there th**at they met a great Spartan** force, and within a week 170 s**hips were sunk and over 4,000** soldiers slain.

In the spring of **404 B.C., Athens surrendere**d.

The terms of surrender involved the loss of the Athenian empire and the destruction of the City walls.

The Spartans set up a Spartan governor and filled the Athenian Council with conservatives of oligarchial leanings.

On top of this, a special supreme governing body of thirty pro-Spartan oligarchs was established. Their leader, Critias, was Plato's uncle and a former follower of Socrates. (Plato remembered these days in his Seventh Letter.)

At first, Plato was pleased to see his uncle Critias take control. He hoped that the leaders would restore order after years of "mob rule" (participatory democracy).

But they soon became known as the Thirty Tyrants, and they ruled the City with terror for over a year (c. 404—403 B.C.). Many prominent citizens and resident foreigners were killed or forced into exile.

Plato became an unwilling associate of the regime.

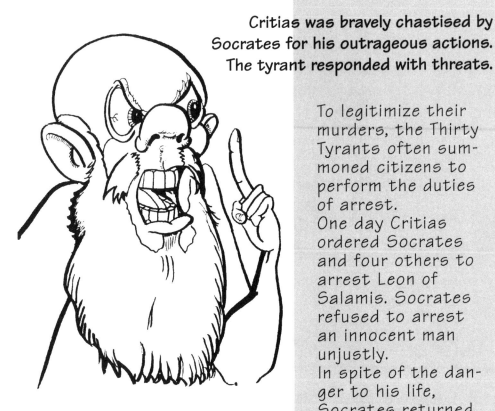

Critias was bravely chastised by Socrates for his outrageous actions. The tyrant responded with threats.

To legitimize their murders, the Thirty Tyrants often summoned citizens to perform the duties of arrest.
One day Critias ordered Socrates and four others to arrest Leon of Salamis. Socrates refused to arrest an innocent man unjustly.
In spite of the danger to his life, Socrates returned quietly home.

Soon a revolt broke out against the Thirty Tyrants. The leaders of the democratic forces included a man called Anytus.

In 403 B.C., the leaders of the regime were driven out of the City and killed.

Sparta, no longer fearing Athens and more concerned with her own problems, stayed out of the battle. By 402 B.C., democracy was again restored.

Once victory was theirs, the democratic forces acted with great restraint; despite the death of his uncle, Plato was impressed with the moderation of the restored democracy.

Peace had again returned to the city-state of Athens.

In the years that followed the restored democracy, a mood of anxious reassessment settled upon Athens. There was a general crisis of the spirit, and people were asking what had gone wrong.

How could Athens have declined so much in the last century? Where were the gods who had guided the Athenians in their victory against the Persians? Were the mortals to blame? What kind of disease had entered the City? What corruption had taken place, and who was responsible for it?

And they saw one man above all others who appeared to represent the very essence of the disease: They saw Socrates as the very source of Athens' ills!

Plato is now seen as a constant companion of Socrates.

When certain thoughtful and pious men looked about, they perceived that a change had begun with the arrival of the philosophers and the Sophists (with their questioning of the gods and of traditional values). It was here that these men saw the source of the disease, the disease that resulted in impiety and the corruption of the youth.

Was not Socrates seen as an atheist and Sophist in The Clouds?

Were not those who followed him anti-democratic aristocrats like Plato?

Had not the notorious Alcibiades been his lover?

Had not the atheist and tyrant Critias been his disciple?

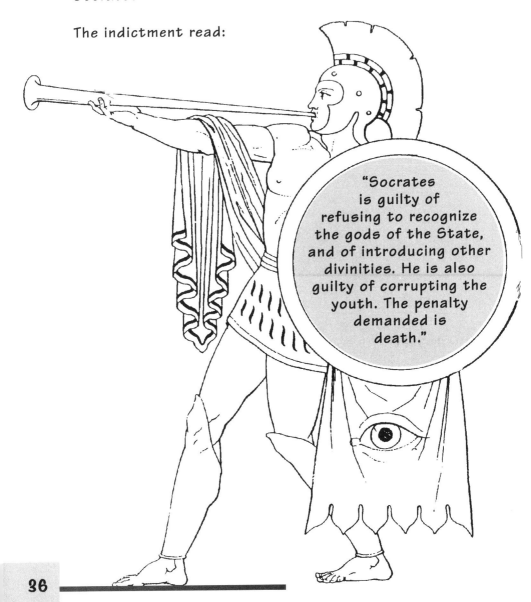

So might have thought Anytus, a leader of the revolt against the Thirty.

At any rate, in 399 B.C., Anytus, Meletus (a relatively unknown poet and religious fanatic), and Lycon (an orator) received from the courts of Athens an indictment against Socrates.

The indictment read:

"Socrates is guilty of refusing to recognize the gods of the State, and of introducing other divinities. He is also guilty of corrupting the youth. The penalty demanded is death."

THE TRIAL
OF
SOCRATES

"I'm like a gadfly who's always buzzing about, bothering horses and preventing them from becoming sluggish and going to sleep — only I buzz around the town making sure no one thinks they know something when they really don't!"

After hearing his defense, a vote is taken — and Socrates is found guilty by a margin of some 30 votes.

In Athenian courts a person found guilty was permitted to offer an alternative penalty to the one proposed by those who brought the charges.

Socrates shocked everyone when he proposed that he receive free meals for the rest of his life!

There is a great uproar, and Socrates offers some money instead (Plato and other wealthy friends of Socrates up the ante to the equivalent of several hundred dollars).

A VOTE IS TAKEN BY AN OVERWHELMING MARGIN, AND THE OFFENDED ATHENIANS GIVE SOCRATES THE DEATH PENALTY.

Socrates in still in jail — the journey of a sacred ship delays his execution some 30 days.

Two days before the ship arrives, his old friend Crito comes to visit Socrates and tells him that arrangements have been made for his escape.

Socrates is not persuaded by Crito's appeal to the opinion that anyone in Socrates' situation would certainly take advantage of this opportunity. **He points out to Crito that it's not living that's important, but living rightly.** Since Socrates made an agreement to abide by the Laws of Athens, and since he feels the Laws are not to blame for his wrongful conviction, it would not be right for him to break those Laws by escaping from jail... .

THE DEATH OF SOCRATES

To the dismay of his student and friends, Socrates insists on drinking the poisonous hemlock as his sentence demands.

Plato recounted the last moments of his mentor in the Phaedo.

The trial and death of Socrates profoundly alienated Plato. Any remaining desires for a political career were now crushed.

Plato left Athens for Megara. Here he and several other friends of Socrates gathered at the invitation of Euclides. It was a time of mourning and consolation.

From Megara, Plato travelled to Egypt and Cyrene.

But by 395 B.C., he was back in Athens and riding with the Athenian cavalry. He was even decorated for valor.

YET ALL THIS WHILE PLATO WAS THINKING OF SOCRATES AND THE PHILOSOPHICAL PROBLEMS THAT HAD CONCERNED HIS FRIEND....

HE WAS CONVINCED THAT SOCRATES HAD LIVED A NOBLE AND WORTHWHILE LIFE. YET HE SAW THAT BY THE STANDARDS OF HIS DAY, *THAT* LIFE HAD BEEN LIVED AND ENDED IN A DISGRACEFUL WAY.

He no doubt felt the need to justify the life of Socrates.

Already there were those who claimed to be continuing to follow Socrates. But Plato felt that they had completely misunderstood Socrates...

Aristippus:

Antisthenes:

IT'S ALL POVERTY!

It's all Pleasure!

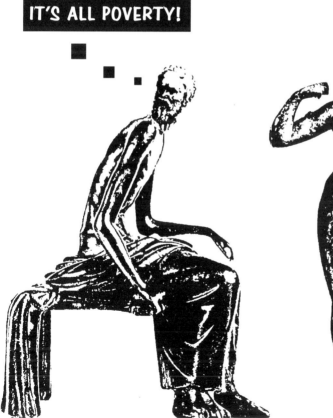

He wrote the Apology.

He also wrote "dialogues" that mirrored the kind of situations and conversations that Socrates might have actually had — e.g., Lysis (about love), Euthyphro (about piety), Crito (about civil disobedience). These and other works became known as the "early dialogues."

(By the way, writing "apologies" and Socratic dialogues was quite in vogue for a while. Xenophon wrote some, and even the cobbler Simon tried his hand at a few.)

BUT PLATO SAW THAT THE LIFE OF SOCRATES COULD NEVER BE JUSTIFIED UNLESS HE COULD SOMEHOW PROVE IT WAS THE BEST SORT OF LIFE FOR EVERYONE.

It so happened that the very year that Socrates was executed, a tyrant to the north (named Archelaus) was murdered by his boy friend while on a hunting trip.

Archelaus had lived a ruthless and unjust life, and yet he was "successful" by the standards of his day. His life served Plato as a useful contrast to that of Socrates, as we shall see.

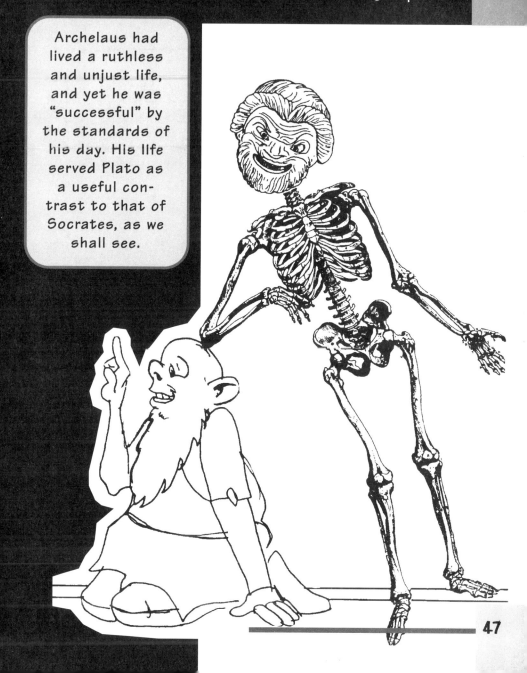

Plato's goal was to show that Socrates' life (the life of the philosopher) is the best way of life — and this is so if it can be shown that this life is grounded in the TRUTH.

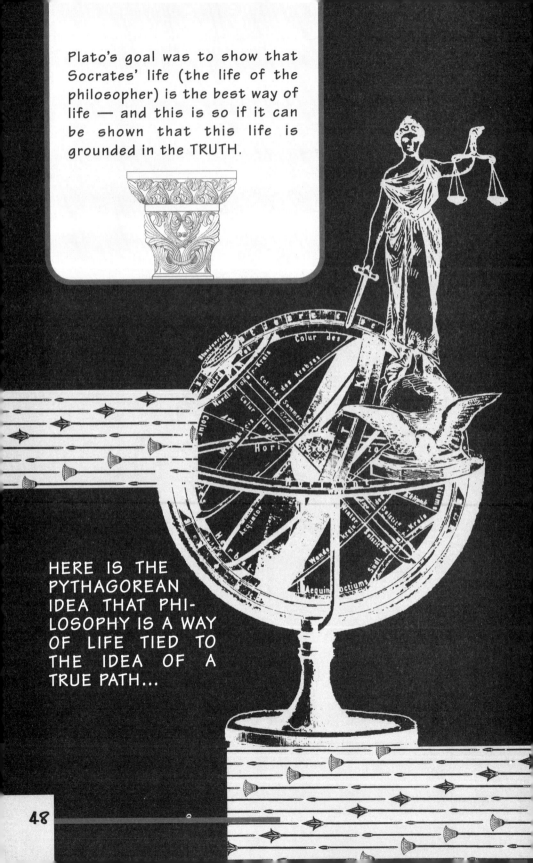

HERE IS THE PYTHAGOREAN IDEA THAT PHILOSOPHY IS A WAY OF LIFE TIED TO THE IDEA OF A TRUE PATH...

To find this "true path," Plato would have to move beyond the thought of his mentor — for Socrates never claimed to have absolute and certain knowledge of things such as truth, justice, and goodness.

But where was such knowledge to be found? Certainly not in the world around him — here there was only opinion, uncertainty and skepticism.

The movement beyond Socrates is basically the **Theory of the Forms.** The Forms are supersensible realities that provide a firm ground for all our beliefs. If I have an opinion about numbers, my opinion is verified when I "see" the truth. If I have an opinion about justice, my opinion is verified when I "see" the true and absolute **FORM** of Justice itself.

It is in this Realm of the Forms (a Reality that can only be seen through the eye of the mind) that all truth is to be found!

Listen, this is what I mean, and this is what I am going to try to prove to you in my dialogues about the Forms...

When we talk about something, and when we claim that we know what we are talk-ing about, there is a whole cluster of things going on. Let me untangle that clus-ter and show you what I mean when I say that someone really knows something.

Take the example of a circle. What's really going on in claiming to know what a "circle" really is?

FIRST, there is something called a "circle."

The word circle is one of the things that is involved when we speak about circles.

But a real circle is something quite different from the English word "circle," the Spanish word "circulo" or the Greek word "cyclos," etc.

Hence a knowledge about a circle is not a knowledge about the "word" circle; a real circle is different from the letters "c-i-r-c-l-e."

SECOND, one may give a description of a circle such as "that which Is everywhere equidistant from the extremities to the center."

But since this description is still in terms of words, it is not the same as the "real thing" to which these words are referring.

And besides, how do you know that the description is a true description?

THIRD, sometimes we try to show what we mean by drawing a picture or by giving an example.

There are pictures of circles on this page, and you see them by "looking" at them (i.e., by perceiving them through the senses).

But for Plato these "objects" are never the same as the real thing.

They are, at best, imperfect approximations (a true straight line can never be drawn). And furthermore, these images can be erased — but the real nature of a circle can never be "erased."

Circles would still exist even if no one ever saw one.

Hence, a **real circle** is distinct from all particular (imperfect and changing) instances of it.

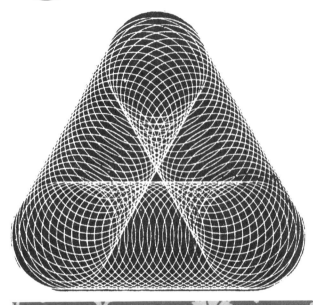

And besides, how do you know that the example (instance) is a correct example? Here's an example of a triangle: Or is it?

(And we don't get our knowledge of these things from a teacher or a book — for how do we know that what they say is the truth?
Believing what they say is different from knowing that what they see is in fact correct!)

In thinking about all of this, Plato came to realize that our knowledge of things did not rest on words, descriptions, or images — much less authority.

All right, where is knowledge to be found?

Plato saw that when we claim to know what a circle is we are speaking about understanding what a circle is — and understanding does not refer to sounds or shapes but to something in the mind.

The **mind** provides the clue to the problem of knowledge!

Plato argues that when we have a true knowledge of what a circle actually is, we do not have a mere knowledge of words or a perception of an image, but rather we have some sort of intellectual grasp of the true nature of the circle in and of itself.

And Plato calls this intellectual grasp of the true nature of a circle a real knowledge of the true **Form of the Circle.**

THE FORM OF THE CIRCLE IS WHAT THE CIRCLE TRULY IS....

If you don't have this, perhaps you don't really know what a circle is. Perhaps you only have an opinion gathered from your teachers! But Plato wants everyone to be able to grasp the true nature (or Form) of a circle for themselves.

Furthermore, Plato contends that this kind of analysis can and must be done for all the things that matter to us when we speak with one another....

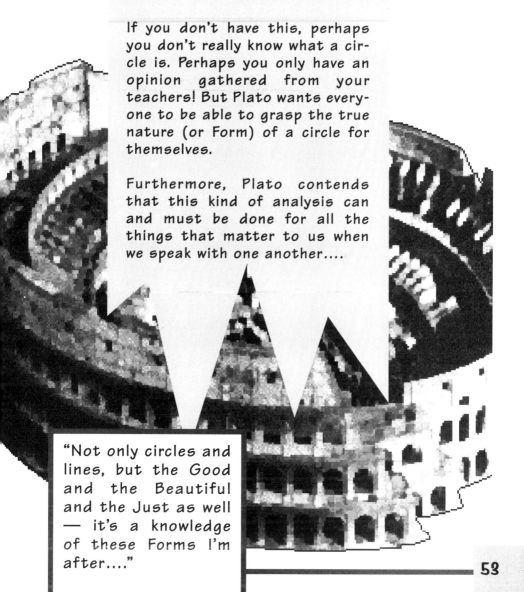

"Not only circles and lines, but the Good and the Beautiful and the Just as well — it's a knowledge of these Forms I'm after...."

If the life of Socrates is to be defended, Plato has to show that he did in fact live a good life, and that the good life is also the best life for everyone to live.

"But to prove this I'll need more than the word 'good' (for what does this mean?) and more than simply pointing to Socrates (for others would point to Archelaus as an example of the Good life)."

"We must have an intellectual grasp of the nature of Goodness itself before we can 'see' how Socrates (and not Archelaus) lived the truly Good life. Only then can we go on to judge whether that life is also the best life."

"But first I have to prove my point about the Forms. Once they have been shown to exist, everything else will fall into place. For example, if I know what Goodness is, then I can compare the life of Socrates with the Form of the Good and know for certain whether Socrates really did live the Good life (as for this being also the best life, that's another matter)."

"AND IF THERE IS A FORM OF JUSTICE, THEN I CAN BUILD A JUST CITY MODELED UPON THE FORM OF JUSTICE ITSELF."

MY PHILOSOPHY IS AS NECESSARY FOR THE STATE AS IT IS FOR THE INDIVIDUAL... ."

One way to understand what Plato means by the "Forms" is to follow him on the "PATH OF KNOWLEDGE."

55

THE THEAETETUS

An elderly Socrates, a middle-aged mathematician named Theodorus, a freshly oiled look-a-like of Socrates, and a group of others are standing about arguing over just what knowledge is....

Theaetetus suggests that knowledge is the same as sense perception (i.e., you "know" something when you see it, taste it, etc.). Socrates peers into Theaetetus' suggestion...

Theaetetus: Knowing it is looking at it, feeling it, tasting it, hearing it, smelling it....

Socrates: So knowing is perceiving....Well, that's what the Sophist Protagoras would say too.

CONSIDER A BUCKET OF WATER... One person who has just come in from the cold, after putting her hand in the water, will say with absolute certainty, "This water is warm!"

Question: Who's to know who is right?

Protagoras: No one can — they're both right. Each is right because each can't be "wrong" about what they feel.

Sensation and knowledge, at this level, are relative to each perceiver.

When applied to sense perception, Protagoras' saying "Man is the measure of all things" means:

(1) Each person is absolutely sure of his/her immediate sensations (so each is the measure...);

(2) Different people might feel (know) different sensations — even from the "same thing" at the same time.

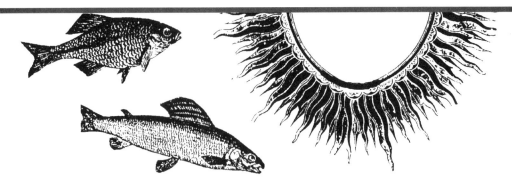

HERACLITUS, c.550 B.C., claimed that "Everything flows." Like a flame, Being is constantly changing.

ALL THE THINGS THAT WE PERCEIVE THROUGH THE SENSES ARE IN CONSTANT FLUX AND CHANGE.

The flowing river that we once saw (knew) a minute ago has "changed" since then — it is not the "same" river that we once knew. (The stick floating downstream has moved, the water has moved, the fish have moved — and some have been eaten.) This doctrine applies to apparently "stationary" objects as well.

Suppose we apply the Protagorean and Heraciltean doctrines to other areas of knowledge beyond sense perception.

THE EXTREME PROTAGOREAN DOCTRINE:
"MAN IS THE MEASURE OF ALL THINGS."

Question: What happens when we apply this doctrine not only to sensations like hot and cold, sweet and sour, but also to our thoughts about what is beautiful and ugly, right and wrong, just and unjust, true and false, etc.?

Protagoras: Each person becomes the final judge of what is to be considered beautiful and ugly or true and false — all these notions become relative to, for example, the individual or his tribe.

THE EXTREME HERACILTEAN DOCTRINE:
"EVERYTHING IS IN A STATE OF FLUX."

Heraclitus: When applied to all possible realities, there is nothing that is not in a state of perpetual change and flux. Individuals change their opinions about what is beautiful or good. What at one time is considered true (e.g., that the world is flat), at another time is considered false (e.g., the world is round).

Consequence: Opinions about beauty and justice are not only relative (Protagoras) but also continually changing (Heraclitus).

> THE EXTREME DOCTRINES DENY THE POSSIBILITY OF ANY ABSOLUTE TRUTH AND KNOWLEDGE IN THESE MATTERS.

The consequences of these extreme positions horrified Plato. He had no problem with relativity in the realm of the senses — in fact, he supported this belief. But he refused to accept the possibility that there is relativity in our thoughts about Truth, Beauty, Justice, etc.

So Socrates goes on the attack...

CRITICISM OF THE EXTREME PROTAGOREAN DOCTRINE

(A) Do we really believe that right and wrong, true and false, etc. are simply "relative" to each person? In that case, why don't we take a sick child to a carpenter instead of to a doctor, if each is "the measure of truth?" (In fact, we go to doctors at such time because they know more than carpenters about these matters. In the same sense, we have carpenters, not doctors, build our house.)

(B) If "truth is relative to each person," then it would follow that whatever anyone said would be true, and so nothing could be "false." The person who says "Protagoras' doctrine is mistaken" would be saying something true!

Protagoras: "There is no absolute truth!"

Socrates: "Is that true?"

Protagoras: "It's absolutely true!"

Socrates: "Hmm... ."

CRITICISM OF THE EXTREME HERACLITEAN DOCTRINE

If everything were really in a state of constant flux, we wouldn't even be able to talk with one another. For example, if "apple" meant at one moment "red fruit, " and at another moment "hairy animal," we wouldn't be able to communicate — we would never know what the other person was meaning (or even what we mean from moment to moment). We couldn't even speak about a "doctrine of the flux."

The extreme doctrines end in inconsistency and incoherence. But these doctrines do seem to account for sense perception. Now, is this sense perception really knowledge?

All we seem to get from the senses is a constant flux of infallible sensations that are relative to each person. This can hardly be called knowledge at all! And, furthermore, most "objects" of knowledge aren't even in the realm of the senses. Truth and Justice aren't to be found there. Even notions such as Difference and Sameness don't come from the senses.

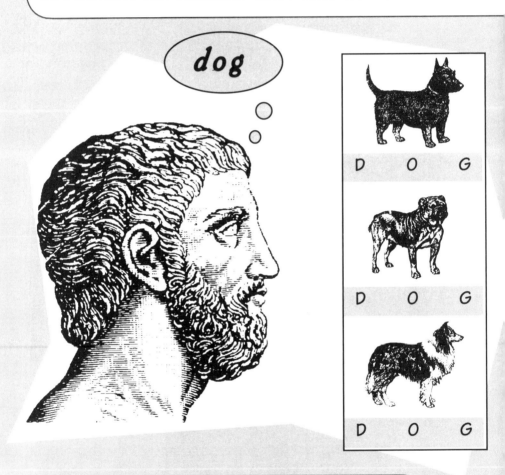

dog

D O G

D O G

D O G

While we "see" these objects through the senses, we judge their differences through the mind (and this is where real knowledge is to be found).
So we're back to the mind as the place where real knowledge occurs. Socrates has tested Theaetetus' idea that knowledge is to be found in sense perception and has found it to be false.

THE SOPHIST

Socrates, Theodorus, Theaetetus, and others are joined the next day by a Stranger from Elea. They are in the middle of a search for the nature of the Sophist. For Plato, the Sophist is a person who can appear to know everything when in fact he knows nothing with absolute truth.

The Sophist merely persuades others of his opinions — and claims that he can teach others to do the same.

We can only understand what true knowledge is when we understand the true Nature of Reality.

Now there are two opinions about Reality, and they are constantly in conflict with one another.

These opinions can be seen in the
THE GIANTS VS. THE GODS

THE GIANTS

This motley group, titanic and rude, represents the hard core materialists. The only realm of reality is the realm of material objects (rocks, trees, clubs, pots and pans, special sales at Simon's Sandal Shop, etc.). For this group, it's only real if you can kick it or wear it. They believe only in things that they can crush with their hands.

For the giants, the material realm is the only realm that exists.

THE GODS

This divine group, dwelling in a place beyond the realm of physical objects, represents the hard core idealists. For them, the only realm of reality is the realm of ideal objects — objects like the number "2" (which is separate from any pair of material objects like two shoes) or the idea of Beauty (which is separate from any landscape or person).

For the gods, the ideal realm is the
only realm that exists

For Plato, there's a truth in both positions.

The materialists satisfactorily account for sensation (relative, changing reality) — through the Heraclitean **Principle of Becoming**. But to explain ultimate reality, Plato adapts the Parmenidean **Principle of Forms**—representing ideal and unchanging reality—to a new use.

Putting both the realm of sensible things and the realm of the Forms together, Plato gives us a picture of

THE WHOLE OF REALITY:

THOUGHT AND KNOWLEDGE	∼	in The Realm of the Forms	∼	The Changeless (The Parmenidean Principle of Being)
SENSATION AND BELIEF	⌘	in The Realm of Sensible Things	⌘	The Changing (The Heraclitean Principle of Becoming)

The problem of knowledge is solved! Reality actually has two levels, and it's only on the second level (the level of the Forms) that we find a place for knowledge. True knowledge is knowledge of the Forms.

It's this picture that moves Plato beyond all his predecessors. For instance, the Physicalists were merely interested in understanding the nature of sensible objects, the Sophists denied the existence of any absolute knowledge, and Socrates himself could only raise questions.

In a sense, all the others were looking in the wrong direction. The point is to look upward to the realm of unchanging Forms — and you do this, not by using the senses, but by using the mind alone. The task is to use pure thought to grasp the essential form of, say, Piety or Beauty or Justice.

Once you have grasped the essential form of Piety itself, then you will be able to judge whether a particular action is truly pious or not. Once you have grasped he essential form of Beauty itself, then you will be able to judge whether something in particular is beautiful or not. In other words, only when you have understood with your mind the Forms of Piety and Beauty will you have a true knowledge of Piety and Beauty.

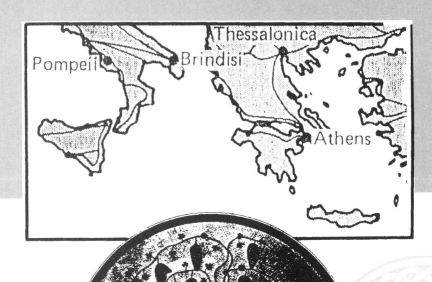

While Plato was busily working out the nature of Reality, history was marching on. In the years since Socrates' death, Athens had become a prosperous commercial port, and Sparta proved inept as a world leader. Throughout the mainland the endless bickering of the city-states with each other continued more or less unabated.

In 387 B.C., a general peace was once again attempted. It was as this period of peace was taking shape that Plato set sail for southern Italy (388-7 B.C.). His travel there was like a pilgrimage to the land of one of his favorite philosophers — the mystic-mathematician Pythagoras.

Pythagoras of Samos was profoundly influenced by the Orphic religion — the only cult that ever threatened the Greek world with the establishment of a ruling priesthood. The Orphic cult of Dionysos contained elements of reincarnation, mystical metaphysics and orgiastic worship. Plato was clearly open to some of its notions, notably asceticism, and salvation through metaphysical understanding.

Pythagoras himself claimed to recall former lives and held that the soul is a fallen divinity trapped in material incarnations. He made numerous mathematical discoveries in geometry and music, possibly including the "Pythagorean theorum."

The Pythagoreans also had an extensive cosmology including a round earth and an "anti-earth" that accounted for eclipses. In the late sixth century B.C., Pythagoras and his followers dominated the Greek city of Croton in southern Italy, where for over 50 years they conducted philosophic inquiries and ran the government. The were finally ousted by a democratic movement about 450 B.C. By Plato's time, exiled Pythagoreans had returned to the region and settled at Tarentum.

Accordingly, Plato visited Tarentum, where he met the Pythagorean philosopher Archytas. Not only a philosopher, Archytas was an accomplished statesmen and general. The same age as Plato, he was already a leader in his city-state. The two men struck up a strong and lasting friendship. And it was here that he also saw the example of a moderate and philosophical ruler.

ON THE AGENDA OF EVERY TRAVELER TO ITALY WERE THE VOLCANOES IN SICILY, AND OF LATE, THERE WAS ALSO SYRACUSE.

Here a man named Dionysius had made the city-state a strong military and political power.

An eccentric and often vicious tyrant, Dionysius nevertheless had a great passion for poetry and the writing of tragedy.

Not only concerned with solidifying his own power, he tried to build Syracuse into a commercial and cultural center. Under his rule this city-state, while not well respected, became well known throughout the Greek world.

When Plato arrived at the court of Dionysius, he was, at first, well received. In fact, he became a mentor to the tyrant's young brother-in-law, Dion (aged 20).

BUT WHILE INFLUENCING DION THROUGH HIS DIS-CUSSIONS OF PHILOSOPHY, HIS BARBS AT TYRANNY ANGERED DIONYSIUS.

Plato soon fell out of favor. He was asked to leave the country on a ship that was taking a Spartan envoy back to central Greece.

Now a remarkable series of events happens...

The ship was probably attacked by pirates. Plato was taken prisoner, and it was decided that he should be sold as a slave.
The sale took place at Aegina. Luckily, a friend of Plato's was in the crowd. He purchased Plato and paid for the philosopher's way back to Athens.

STORY HAS IT THAT WHEN PLATO WAS SAFELY BACK AT ATHENS, HE WANTED TO REPAY HIS FRIEND BUT THE FRIEND REFUSED.

Plato then took the money he had gathered and purchased a small grove just outside the city. The grove was dedicated to a hero named "Hecademos," and it was here (in 387 B.C.) that Plato founded his school —

THE ACADEMY.

As the first "college," the Academy was an organized society with Plato at the head, several advanced students as fellow teachers and a group of students (including women).

The format of the school was one of discussion, and the topics were far ranging — from astronomy to botany. But a central purpose of all the studies was to perfect the skills of analysis and definition.

The comic poet Epicrates mimics this in one of his plays:

" Tell me about Plato and Speuspippus and Menedemus. What are they doing now?...."

"They were defining and dividing up the world of nature...."

"And what did they decide that plant to be?...."

"Well, at first they all stood silent and bent over it for some time considering. Then suddenly...one of the boys said it was a round vegetable, and another said it was a weed, and another said it was a tree... . A Sicilian doctor who was there exploded at the nonsense they were talking... . But that didn't worry the boys. Plato told them very kindly to start over from the beginning... ."

Do not enter unless you know geometry.

The point of this analysis was, for Plato, bound up with the serious attempt at philosophy. The Academy was, after all, a school of philosophy.

Of great importance was the study of mathematics — to such an extent that over the school hung this sign: "Do not enter unless you know geometry."

Here again the purpose of studying mathematics was to free the mind to be able to study philosophy. And the ultimate goal of all purely philosophical studies was the study of the Forms.

THE PATH OF LOVE

Plato continued developing his theory of the Forms. He tried to show how necessary some realm of permanence was for understanding both the world and ourselves.

He burned with passion over these Forms, and thought of them at times as existing in a realm beyond the cosmos, a realm that can only be reached by the mind — the pilot of the soul.

He saw in this passion a way in which the Forms can be made accessible to those who may not start with problems of knowledge.

It was a way that was open to any mortal who experienced what the Greeks called EROS.

To understand how the theory of the Forms can relate to the notion of Eros (or love), we have to realize that for Plato the activity of Eros can excite the soul and create within it a desire to move upward. This upward movement of the soul, provoked by Eros, can somehow lead to the soul's complete transport into the realm of the Forms.

How this movement toward the Forms can occur, and what the soul sees when it reaches the realm of the Forms, are the matters to be explored on THE PATH OF LOVE.

THE PHAEDRUS

Socrates and a beautiful young man named Phaedrus are in the country, sitting under a tree by the river Illissus. Socrates is describing the nature and form of the soul.

The soul is immortal. It has no beginning and no end. Its nature is to be in a state of self-movement.

This self-movement has the form of "a winged chariot and a charioteer."

The charioteer represents the rational part of the soul. Of the two horses, one is a white horse that represents spiritedness and the other is a dark horse that represents desire. The wings indicate that it is proper for the self-movement of the soul to have a natural tendency upward. This upward tendency is to enable to soul to gaze upon the eternal Forms.

For instance, rather that to stay with earthly instances of beauty and justice, the natural tendency of the "unencumbered soul" is to gaze upon the Forms of Beauty and Justice themselves and to try to discover what they really are.

A truly "unencumbered soul" is best seen by looking at the souls of the gods — more specifically, by seeing what the souls of the gods do when they are feasting upon the Forms. (Plato thought of the Forms as the natural "nourishment" for the rational part of the soul.)

Socrates draws a picture of the legions of the gods, led by Zeus, moving upward toward the outer vault of the heavens. Here they gaze beyond the cosmos and upon the eternal Forms:

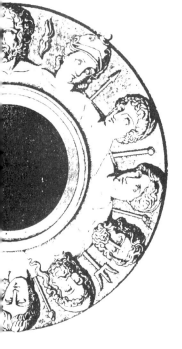

"When they go to a feast or banquet, they proceed to the top of the vault of heaven...and when they reach the top they pass outside and take their place on the outer surface of the heavens and when they have taken their stand, the revolution carries them round and they behold the things beyond the heavens."

"It
i s
t h e r e
that true
Being dwells,
without color
or shape, that
cannot be touched;
reason alone, the
soul's pilot can behold it,
and all true knowledge is
knowledge thereof...In the revolution the soul beholds universal Justice, Virtue, Knowledge, not
such knowledge that has a beginning
and varies...but that which abides in the
real, eternal absolute." (Phaedrus 247c-e)

**The Forms are described as being
beyond the physical (i.e., not accessible
to sense perception) and hence as color-
less, figureless, and intangible.**

YET IT IS ONLY WITH A KNOWLEDGE OF THE
FORMS THAT WE HAVE TRUE KNOWLEDGE. AND
THIS KIND OF KNOWLEDGE CAN BE GAINED ONLY
THROUGH THE USE OF REASON OR MIND.

A final mark of the Forms is that they are **eternal and absolute**. Like the true number "2," which always remains after all physical pairs of twos (two apples, two sand dunes) come and go, so too the Forms of Beauty and Justice remain permanent and unchanging throughout all time.

HENCE, TRUE KNOWLEDGE IS NOT RELATIVE. IT HOLDS FOR ALL PEOPLES AT ALL TIMES — IT IS ABSOLUTE.

The gods, with their divine rational nature, understand these matters easily. Humans can also understand these matters, since part of their nature is also divine (this is the part of the soul called *Reason*). However, with human souls there is more of a struggle.

After discussing the souls of the gods, Socrates turns next to the life of the human soul.

Human souls also appear among the legions that travel to the outskirts of heaven and gaze upon the Forms.

But their dark horse is a problem. It causes much trouble for an unskilled and untrained charioteer. The horse tends to go out of control (trying as it does to move downward), and as a result the wings of most human souls are broken. This causes the chariot and charioteer to plummet downward and become embodied in a mortal living creature! For Plato, this means that the human soul has a pre-existence.

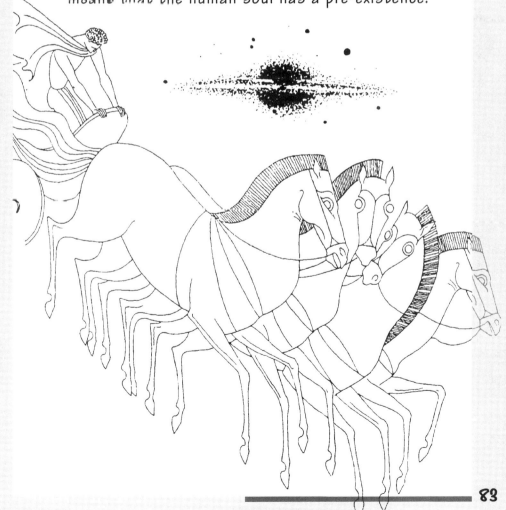

SOCRATES' STORY IS AN ACCOUNT OF HOW WE WE EVENTUALLY BECOME MORTAL HUMAN BEINGS!

It is Plato's adaptation of the Orphic/Pythagorean doctrine of reincarnation. (In the story, it is the destruction of the wings that causes us to become "entombed" in the body!)

One result of reincarnation is Plato's doctrine that all true knowledge involves recollection — for when we achieve true knowledge we are in fact "remembering" our former feast upon the Forms.

This is how the unskilled slave in the Meno is able to "discover" certain mathematical formulas — he was really "recollecting" his prior experience of the eternal Forms of Numbers.

Toward the end of his speech, Socrates tells Phaedrus how this story of the soul and its relation to the Forms is bound up with the activity of Eros.

In true love, the souls of the lover and the beloved are excited in the presence of each other:

"As he looks upon the beloved, a reaction from his shuddering comes over him, with sweat and unwonted heat; for as the stream of beauty enters through his eyes, he is warmed; the effluence moistens the germ of the feather, and as he grows warm, the parts from which the feathers grow...become soft and ... the quills of the feathers swell and begin to grow...."

**TRUE
LOVE
LEADS
TO
A
GROWING
OF
THE
WINGS!**

It is as if the image of a beautiful object awakens in us a past in which we stood with the gods and feasted upon the Form of the Beautiful itself!

The activity of Eros is so great that, properly followed, it can cause the wings of the mortal human soul to grow and once again move upward toward the realm of the Forms.

And if this love is correctly cultivated, it will provoke a desire in the lover and the beloved to move beyond the particular instance of beauty that they now see — and to gaze upon the **Beautiful Itself**.

"He who...sees a godlike face or scene which is a good image of beauty, shudders at first, and something of the old awe comes over him."

But not all people have such an understanding of Eros. In the next dialogue, Plato continues to explore the relation between love and the Forms.

This symposium is a feast given at the house of Agathon to celebrate the victory of his tragedy at the dramatic competitions.

Among those present, and reclining in a semi-circle, are Phaedrus, Aristophanes, and a sandal-wearing Socrates. They begin to give a series of speeches in praise of Eros.

The Symposium The Symposium The Symposium The Symposium

LOVE IS A GREAT GOD, FOR IT HAS THE POWER TO PROVOKE US TO PERFORM GREAT AND NOBLE DEEDS. TO PROVE THIS, PHAEDRUS RECOUNTS HOMER'S STORY OF ACHILLES AND PATROCLES.

Achilles, knowing that he would die if he sought to rescue the body and avenge the death of his lover, Patrocles, courageously slew Hector and thus sealed his own death. He preferred this noble deed, inspired by his love, to the cowardly act which would have stemmed from a concern for his own life.

The Speech Of Aristophanes

Ariſtophanes

A STORY OF THE ORIGINS OF LOVE.

There were originally three sexes born of the Sun (males), Earth (females) and Moon (hermaphrodites). Each of these three sexes were doubled over and united as a whole:

"Each form of person was round all over with back and side encompassing it in every way; each head had four arms, and legs to match these, and two faces perfectly alike on a cylindrical neck. There was one head to the two faces, which looked opposite ways; there were four ears, two sets of genitals, and all the other parts as may be imagined in proportion."

One day this entire race mounted an attack against the Olympic gods. All three sexes somersaulted up toward Zeus! Zeus was furious with such a show of arrogance. But he didn't want to destroy the entire race.

"I think I can contrive that mortals, without ceasing to exist, shall give over this excess through a lessening of their strength. I propose now to slice every one of them in two, so that while making them weaker we shall also find them more useful by reasons of the greater number."

Being cut in half immediately resulted in the forms of heterosexuality (from the hermaphrodites) and homosexuality (in both male and female forms).

A further consequence of this split (besides the origin of the bellybutton, which was used to seal each wounded half) was that each half began to crave for its other half:

"When our first form had been cut in two, each half in longing for its fellow would come to it again; and then would they fling their arms about each other and in mutual embraces yearn to be bound together." (Symposium 191a)

This is the origin of love, continues Aristophanes, and why human beings are constantly chasing after one another....

The Speech Of Socrates

Socrates begins by telling his audience that the speech they are about to hear was one he himself heard as young man. In a private setting, a beautiful priestess named Diotima initiated him into the true secrets of love...

First, he was told that Eros was not a great god, but a demi-god. That is, Eros is a diamon (spirit) somewhere between a mortal and an immortal.

THE STORY OF THE BIRTH OF EROS

"When Aphrodite was born, the gods made a great feast, and among the company was Resource, the son of Cunning. And when they banqueted, there came Poverty abegging as she might do in an hour of cheer... . Now Resource, grown tipsy with nectar...went into the garden of Zeus, and there, overcome with heaviness, slept. Then Poverty, being of herself so resourceless, devised a scheme of having a child by Resource, and lying down by his side, conceived Eros." (Symposium 203c)

Eros inherited the characteristics of both its parents:

From Poverty, Eros inherited a need, a sense of lacking something. From Resource, it inherited cunning and intelligence.

Together, these qualities show that while Eros lacks the beauty and goodness that it desires, it nevertheless uses its cunning and intelligence to constantly strive after that which it lacks.

Originally Eros provokes a lover to strive after the beauty found in an individual body. But soon an erotic lover comes to desire all beautiful bodies.

Many people stay at this level throughout their youth, but most learn later that there is a deeper beauty in the Soul of the beloved.

AT THIS STAGE THE ACTIVITY OF EROS HAS ALREADY MOVED THE LOVER BEYOND THE REALM OF THE PURELY PHYSICAL.

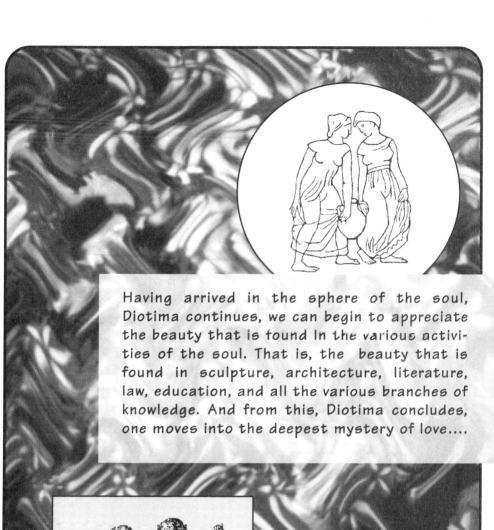

Having arrived in the sphere of the soul, Diotima continues, we can begin to appreciate the beauty that is found In the various activities of the soul. That is, the beauty that is found in sculpture, architecture, literature, law, education, and all the various branches of knowledge. And from this, Diotima concludes, one moves into the deepest mystery of love....

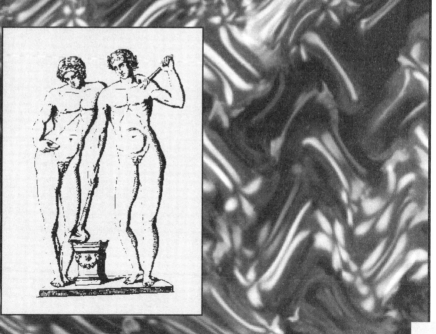

As the lovers begin to appreciate the beauty that can be found in knowledge, they begin to desire the ultimate objects of knowledge.

No longer content to gaze upon particular and passing instances of beauty, the true lover desires to gaze upon the eternal and unchanging form of the BEAUTIFUL ITSELF. This is where erotic desire culminates — in a desire to gaze upon the Forms.

DIOTIMA DESCRIBES THE FORM OF THE BEAUTIFUL AS FOLLOWS:

"First of all, it is ever existent and neither comes to be or passes away...it is not beautiful in part and in any part ugly, nor is it such at such a time and other at another.... Nor again will our initiate find the Beautiful presented to him in the guise of a face or of hands or any other portion of the body, nor as a particular description or a piece of knowledge...he will find it existing forever in a single Form, while all the many different and particular instances of it, while coming to be and passing away, partake by necessity of this single Form without in any manner affecting its eternal and universal state." (SYMPOSIUM 211a-b)

SUMMARY OF THE NATURE OF A FORM
Forms are...

1 ETERNAL— They are without beginning and without end.

2 UNIVERSAL— They are always the same; they are not relative. They are the patterns which form the ideal base of particular beings. Universal Justice is the pattern for worldly justice.

3 KNOWN THROUGH THE MIND (i.e., REASON)—They are not known through the senses. They "exist" in a realm beyond physical reality. Beauty is ultimately an idea, not an object. We must understand what true beauty really is before we can judge a particular object or person to be beautiful or not.

As Socrates finished his recollection, and as applause and comments were being made, a drunken Alcibiades enters the room. Wine is passed around and musicians start to play; the symposium collapses into a Dionysian frenzy.

Let's look a little further into the Forms and the role that they play within the whole of Reality.

Plato gives us his most forceful vision of this in the sections of the Republic known as the DIVIDED LINE and the IMAGE OF THE CAVE.

> WE BEGIN BY DIVIDING THE WHOLE OF REALITY INTO THE "VISIBLE" AND THE "INVISIBLE."

From this general division, we go on to cut each segment into a smaller part of equal proportion.

As we fill in the parts from lower to higher, we are to do so in terms of (a) how we grasp the things on each level and (b) what the things are that we grasp on each level. We are to move upward from the things we imagine and from the images to the things we grasp through the mind or intellect (viz., the Forms).

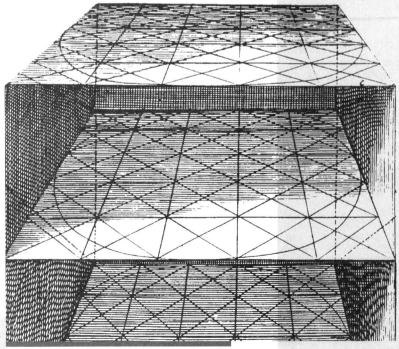

PLATO NEXT GOES ON TO SAY THAT THROUGHOUT THIS HIERARCHICAL PICTURE OF REALITY, THE WHOLE IS GUIDED BY A SINGLE FORM, THE **HIGHEST OF ALL FORMS**.

THIS FORM IS CALLED THE GOOD.

The Form of the Good is the supreme guiding principle of all things. It shines upon the whole as the Sun shines upon the visible. (Republic 508e-509b)

1788 SCHOPENHAUER 1860

If you color "the Good" as "God," you can see how Christianity will eventually take over many of Plato's ideas.

The 19th-century German philosopher, Schopenhauer, once said:

"Christianity is Platonism for the masses."

But how is it that so much of this sounds strange to the ears of the average person?

Plato believed that the structure of Reality was not obvious to everyone because our normal condition is such that we don't see things this way. In fact, our normal condition is similar to that of prisoners held in a cave.

Imagine...

"Men dwelling in a sort of underground cave with a long entrance open to the light on its entire width. Conceive them as having their legs and necks fettered from childhood, so that they remain in the same spot able to look forward only, and prevented by the fetters from turning their heads." (Republic 514a)

Plato continues by describing a burning flame within the cave itself, a flame which casts shadows upon the wall facing the chained prisoners. Between the prisoners and the flame there are image-makers of all sorts, whose creations cause shadows of different shapes to appear before the prisoners' fixed eyes.

Plato wants us to understand that these prisoners are like ourselves. From the moment we are born we see only images and hear only opinions — **but since this is all we ever see, we mistake these passing images and changing opinions for REALITY and TRUE KNOWLEDGE.**

Our human condition is shrouded in darkness and ignorance regarding the ultimate truth of things.

Yet...with some effort it is possible to free ourselves from this condition.

Occasionally a person, through the proper use of reason or through true erotic longing, can turn his or her soul away from the passing shadows and toward the causes of those shadows and beyond.

If one begins such a journey (which could be called "philosophy" or the "love of wisdom"), the path would be difficult and painful.

In the soul's journey upward, the prisoner's eyes, conditioned by a life of darkness, will at first be pained and blinded by what is seen. And yet, once he becomes accustomed to thinking in terms of the "more real things," once he begins to see the various levels of Reality, then he will begin to see everything in the light of the source itself.

From this perspective, the prisoner (now a "freed" man) will see the shadows as shadows and the opinion-makers as what they really are, and he will come to see the "Sun" as the highest and brightest reality.

From such heights outside the Cave, the freeman will be truly happy, and he will take pity on those still in the shadows.

103

As Plato felt that the ascent out of the cave would be painful, so too he warns us that any descent back into the cave (i.e., the world of ordinary life) would be dangerous.

If a "free person" were to return to the shadows and to the men in bondage, he would at first appear to be like a madman, since he would be talking about things that the others can't see. Worse still, the slaves might kill him if he tried to raise doubts about the world around them.

Plato sees in this image of the cave a picture of Socrates. For it is Socrates who represents a true lover of wisdom; it is Socrates who represents the free man turning away from the opinions of others and seeking the truth itself. And it's someone like Socrates who would appear mad or dangerous to those around him.

Yet Plato felt with all his heart that someone like Socrates was on the right track. He saw that his theory of the Forms would guarantee the success of the Socratic search and that, indeed, the realm of the Forms would provide a reward for that search.

SOCRATES PLACED THE HIGHEST VALUE ON KNOWING WHAT THE GOOD LIFE WAS, AND HE WAS CONVINCED THAT IT WAS TO BE FOUND IN A LIFE OF VIRTUE AND KNOWLEDGE.

In Plato's scheme of things, such a life involved a movement upward toward the Forms. This was a movement of the Soul.

The true beauty of Socrates was thus in his soul, not his physical appearance or poverty. (So, too, the true ugliness of a tyrant like Archelaus was in his soul, not in his appearance.)

Elsewhere, Plato speculated that these souls are judged by the gods after death. Those who lived corrupted lives would be punished; those who lived virtuous lives would be rewarded.

So the life of Socrates, spent in pursuit of truth, goodness and justice, was also the best life to live...

It would be a mistake to think that Plato is concerned only with spiritual matters and the individual's intellectual salvation.

There is a decidedly "practical" dimension to the theory of the Forms, and this can be seen more clearly in Plato's political philosophy.

The relationship between the theory of the Forms and politics can be put simply: we should never act without knowledge. So if we wish to build a just city or make just laws, we should only do so after we have understood the meaning of justice. But we cannot achieve an understanding of true justice until we have grasped the Form of Justice itself.

Hence, a knowledge of the Forms is required for political action as well as for personal salvation.

THE REPUBLIC

THE SETTING: the house of the wealthy Cephalus, near the Piraeus. The old man, his son Polemarchus, Plato's brothers Glaucon and Adeimantus, Socrates, Thrasymachus (a Sophist) and others are discussing the problem of justice.

In order to see the problem more clearly, Socrates proposes to talk about justice as it appears in a city-state before going on to justice as it appears in an individual.

In the course of doing so Plato describes what he considers to be an ideal city-state.

As it turns out, this is a Spartan-like society. It is a community of craftsmen, farmers, guardians and guard helpers.

The education of the citizens consists of both MUSIC and GYMNASTICS:

Music is to instill inner harmony, and its purpose is to cultivate the soul of the learner.

Music includes not only sounds and rhythms, but poetry as well. In regard to the latter, the guardians are to allow only carefully censored poetry, i.e., poems that have images that convey impressions of justice and good disposition.

GYMNASTICS IS TO INSTILL PHYSI-
CAL STRENGTH, AND ITS PURPOSE IS
TO CULTIVATE THE BODY OF THE
LEARNER. TOGETHER, THESE ASPECTS
ARE INTENDED TO MAKE THE CITI-
ZEN OF THIS IDEAL CITY-STATE BOTH
MODERATE (HARMONIOUS) AND
COURAGEOUS (STRONG).

...t not all citizens are alike in nature and capabilities — and only those who are best (aristos) in every way should be selected as guardians and as auxiliaries to the guardians of the city-state. (These will be the true "aristocracy.")

Yet how to convince everyone of their differences? And how to do this in such a way that they'll mind their own business and accept their proper place?

At this point Plato has recourse to Noble Lie (i.e., a falsehood that is for the good of everyone). Socrates proposes to instill a myth about human nature that will someday become part of the tradition of an ideal city-state:

THIS MYTH OF THE MIXED METALS ACCOUNTS
FOR THE DIFFERENCES AMONG THE CITIZENS.

It seems that, before we were born, the Earth
(our true mother) fashioned the materials of our
body and nature. But even though this makes us
all brothers and sisters, at our birth she mixed
gold in with those who were to become guardians,
silver in with the auxiliaries, and iron and bronze
in with the farmers and other craftsmen.

These differences are not absolute, for sometimes a farmer's child ascends to a guardian and sometimes a guardian's child descends to a farmer. The result, nevertheless, is a rigid class system of money-makers (the iron and bronze natures of the craftsmen), auxiliaries (silver), and guardians (gold) — with the guardians and the auxiliaries ruling over the money-makers.

The life of the "ruling classes" is to be lived in strict communism:

(1) No one will possess any private property;

(2) Everyone is to live in common housing and is to share in common meals.

By not having a "this is mine" and a "I want yours" in their vocabulary, and by always living in common surroundings, Plato believes that the desire for power will not arise. The result would be that the rulers would always strive for the common good of all.

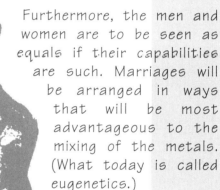

Furthermore, the men and women are to be seen as equals if their capabilities are such. Marriages will be arranged in ways that will be most advantageous to the mixing of the metals. (What today is called eugenetics.)

There is to be no private life between a man and a woman, and the children will be "common," having neither a specific mother nor a specific father. (Like a radical Kibbutz or Skinner's Walden Two.) All the children are to be bred and raised for the common good of all.

What Plato envisioned is nothing less than an "enlightened society." But how do we know that this is the best a city-state can be? And how are the guardians to know that they are doing the right thing?

Plato's answer is that there needs to be a king who has an absolute knowledge of these matters (i.e., a king who has gained a knowledge of the forms of Justice and Goodness).

But this leads to a paradox for a person most capable of such knowledge is not a man of action but a man of contemplation, i.e., a philosopher.

For this city-state to be truly possible, there must arise in it a single person who is both a philosopher and a king. That is to say, Plato's ideal city-state must ultimately be ruled by a PHILOSOPHER-KING!

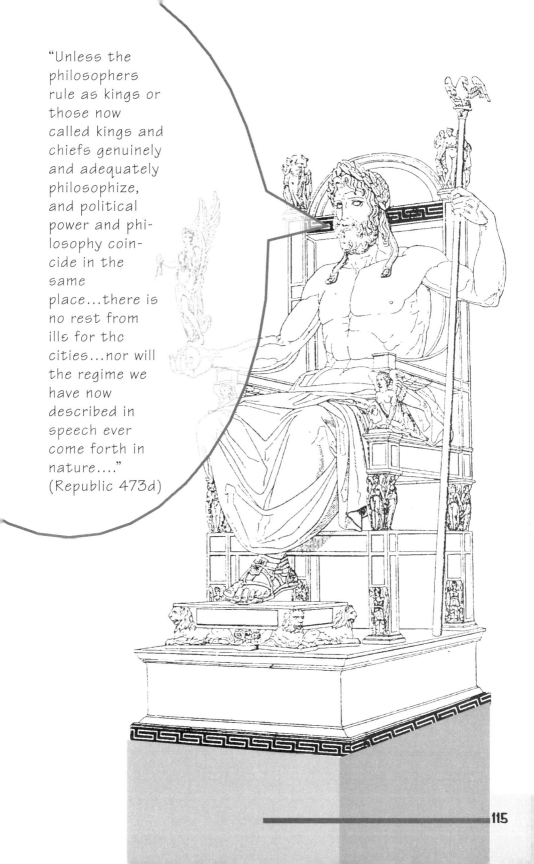

"Unless the philosophers rule as kings or those now called kings and chiefs genuinely and adequately philosophize, and political power and philosophy coincide in the same place...there is no rest from ills for the cities...nor will the regime we have now described in speech ever come forth in nature...." (Republic 473d)

As it turned out, history seemed to be providing Plato with what he needed — a young king whose education might be entrusted to a philosopher.

In 369 B.C., the old tyrant Dionysius had won a prize in the dramatic competitions in Athens. He was so excited by the award that, according to legend, he drank himself to death during the celebrations.

The tyrant left behind a son, Dionysius II, and his most respected minister, Plato's disciple Dion.

THUS IT CAME ABOUT THAT, IN 367 B.C., DION SUMMONED PLATO TO THE COURT FOR THE PURPOSE OF INSTRUCTING THE YOUNG KING.

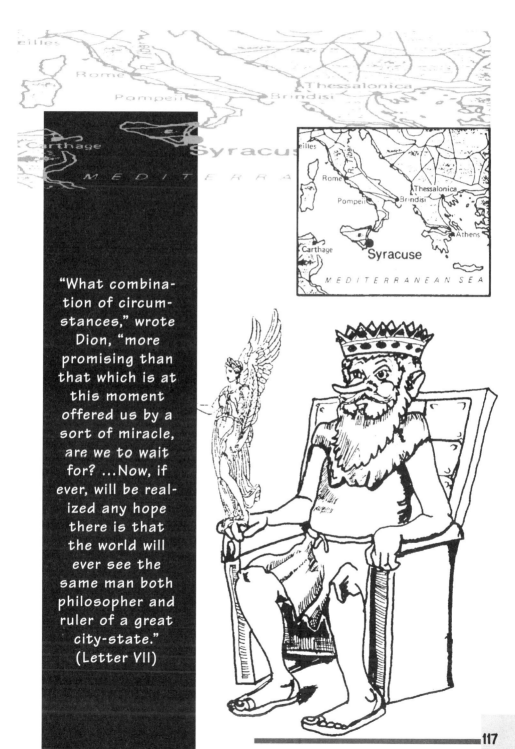

"What combination of circumstances," wrote Dion, "more promising than that which is at this moment offered us by a sort of miracle, are we to wait for? ...Now, if ever, will be realized any hope there is that the world will ever see the same man both philosopher and ruler of a great city-state." (Letter VII)

When Plato arrived at Syracuse he was eager to put his philosophy into action. However, he soon realized that there were factions in the court. Certain parties had suggested to Dionysius that Dion and Plato were involved in a conspiracy against him. Dion was ordered into exile and Plato was forced to remain in the palace.

It was under these strained conditions that Plato and Dionoysius got to know one another. There was no real instruction in philosophy at this time, though Plato did try to convey to the tyrant the importance of attending to one's soul. At last, some degree of mutual respect did grow between them.

But Dionysius was soon involved in a war with Carthage. He asked Plato to leave, saying that when peace had been made, he would send for him again — and he'd allow Dion to return as well.

Four years went by, and in 362 B.C. Dionysius sent a ship for Plato.

At first Plato hesitated, since the offer to Dion had been withdrawn. But his friends convinced him that it would be best to return.

"So I did set out under cover of these arguments, full of fears, as you might well expect, and foreboding no very good results."

Plato's fears were confirmed. Dionysius soon showed impatience with him, and little regard for the rigorous study of philosophy. On top of all this, Dionysius confiscated Dion's property.

Plato was furious and prepared to depart no matter what the consequences. Dionysius, however, fearing embarrassment from the philosopher's departure, made the following proposal:

"Let Dion and Dion's affairs be cleared from our path, that you and I no longer be at variance over them. For your sake, I will do this for Dion. I propose that he receive his property and live in the Peloponnesus ... providing he contrive no plots against me....See whether you find this offer satisfactory. If you do, stay one these terms another year and next season take this money and depart."

So Plato agreed to stay—living under virtual house arrest in a garden belonging to the palace.

But after the season for sailing had passed, Dionysius abruptly sold Dion's property. Further intrigues led Dionysius and Plato once again into conflict, with Dionysius feeling that Plato was involved with Dion in a plot against him. Threats to Plato's life were coming from groups of angered sailors and mercenaries who were loyal to the tyrant.

Fearing for his life, Plato sent a message to his friend Archytas in Tarentum. Archytas sent an emissary to Syracuse and asked that Plato be allowed to depart. Dionysius granted the request and gave Plato some money for travelling expenses. But he refused any comment on Dion.

Plato left Syracuse for the last time in 360 B.C.

Shortly after arriving on the mainland, he met Dion during a festival at Olympia. By this time Dion was indeed plotting the overthrow of Dionysius. Plato, preferring mediation, declined any active participation in the revolt.

THE TIMAEUS

In the Timaeus, a work that is very different from all his other writings, Plato, like the Physicalists, sought to explore THE NATURE OF THE UNIVERSE.

> The setting: Timaeus, a Pythagorean from Italy, is speaking to Socrates, Critias (Plato's notorious uncle), and Hermocrates about the nature of the universe, from its original organization down to the creation of man.

There is a distinction, Timaeus reminds us, between that which is eternal and unchanging and that which is always in a state of change and flux.

IN THE BEGINNING, the material of the visible universe was not only in a state of flux, but it was also utterly unformed and chaotic. At that time, a Divine Craftsman took this chaos and, with an eye toward the eternal Forms, gave matter order and purpose.

THIS IS HOW THE UNIVERSE BECAME A COSMOS (I.E., AN "ORDERED WHOLE"). THE ENTIRE SPHERE OF THE VISIBLE BECAME LIKE A LIVING CREATURE — AND IT WAS ALL FASHIONED FOR A GOOD PURPOSE.

THE ELEMENTS OF THIS VISIBLE COSMOS WERE EARTH, FIRE, AIR, AND **WATER.**

"God fashioned them by form and number...and made them the fairest and best out of things that were not beautiful and good."

These elements, in their simplest ("atomic") appearance, took the following mathematical forms:

(1) **FIRE** (regular tetrahedra)

(2) **AIR** (regular octahedra)

(3) **WATER** (regular icosahedra)

(4) **EARTH** (regular cubes)

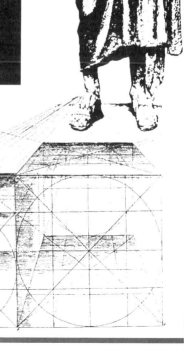

These organized elements, in combination with themselves and with each other, give us the Body of the World.

The shape of the world is a globe, and moving around it, like circles within circles, are the sun, moon, planets, and stars — and the vaults of the heavens.

And because all this was set into motion by the Divine Craftsman, it all partakes of reason and harmony. The Cosmos, Plato and Timeaus proclaim, is by its very nature **rational** and **good**.

First, he made the gods and the children of the gods. To these divine creatures, the Craftsman gave the power to form the bodies of the other living

The gods first made Man, the most divine-like of the animals. And from men there soon arose women and the mingling of the sexes.

Certain men and women, who were by nature innocent and lightminded, were remodeled and turned into birds (growing feathers instead of hair).

The race of wild animals came from dull-witted men and women "who had no philosophy in their thoughts." The duller they were, the closer they were to dragging themselves upon the earth.

Lizards and snakes were thus the lowest kind. But for the most ignorant, there was reserved the race of fish and oysters.

AND TO ALL LIVING SPECIES EXCEPT THE FIRST, THERE WAS TO BE A LAW OF REINCARNATION, WHEREBY "THEY PASS INTO AND OUT OF ONE ANOTHER, CHANGING AS THEY LOSE OR GAIN WISDOM AND FOLLY."

PLATO'S LAST WORK

THE LAWS

Plato did not stay long with the speculations of the Physicalists. And in his last years he turned again to politics. In fact, he took up the role of his great-uncle Solon — **Plato became a lawgiver.**

The resulting dialogue is called the Laws, one of Plato's last works, and it refines and modifies the Republic.

THE SETTING: The location is the island of Crete, with three elderly men (Plato himself as the Athenian Stranger, a Cretan named Kleinias, and a Spartan named Megillus) making a pilgrimage to the cave and temple of Zeus. Kleinias has been charged with founding a new colony, so on the journey the three decide to discuss the laws which might govern this new city-state.

Plato says that the easiest way to organize a new city-state would be to have a moderate tyrant and a good lawgiver (an idealized Dionysius and Dion?) build and secure the city-state and its laws with persuasion and force. And the best regime that could be built would be an idealized communistic society.

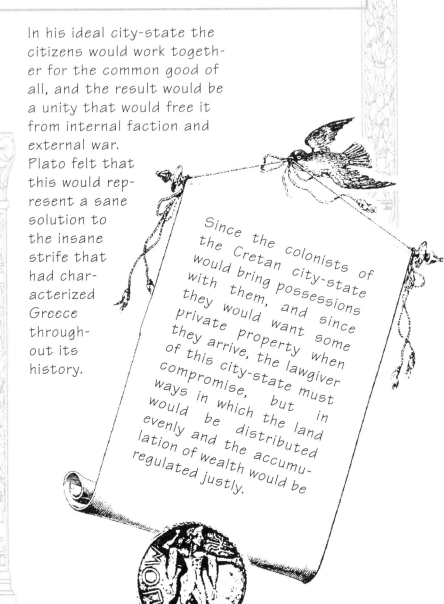

In his ideal city-state the citizens would work together for the common good of all, and the result would be a unity that would free it from internal faction and external war. Plato felt that this would represent a sane solution to the insane strife that had characterized Greece throughout its history.

Since the colonists of the Cretan city-state would bring possessions with them, and since they would want some private property when they arrive, the lawgiver of this city-state must compromise, but in ways in which the land would be distributed evenly and the accumulation of wealth would be regulated justly.

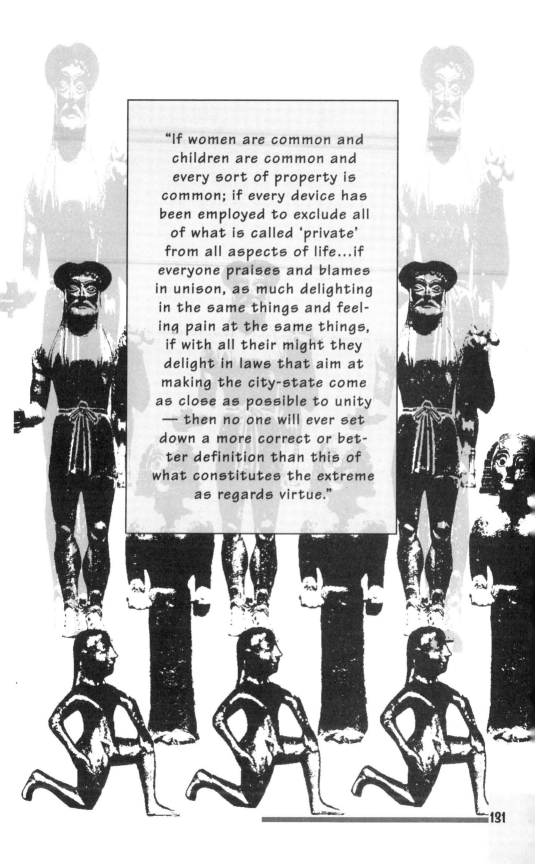

"If women are common and children are common and every sort of property is common; if every device has been employed to exclude all of what is called 'private' from all aspects of life…if everyone praises and blames in unison, as much delighting in the same things and feeling pain at the same things, if with all their might they delight in laws that aim at making the city-state come as close as possible to unity — then no one will ever set down a more correct or better definition than this of what constitutes the extreme as regards virtue."

The land (which is inland, rough, yet productive enouph to be self-sufficient) is divided into 5,040 plots, radiating outward in 12 districts from the central part of town. In the center of the city-state is to be an acropolis (with temples to Hestia, Zeus, and Athena) surrounded by a circular wall. A marketplace and municipal buildings will make up most of the urban center. A plot of land is to be given to each colonist, and it is to remain his and his heirs' unaltered through time.

Further, each share-holder must also recognize that his share is at the same time the common property of the whole city-state. At bottom, this "distribution of land" is designed to create stability in the city-state, since landholders can neither sell off their land (and become reduced to slaves) nor gain large plots (and become an elite upper class).

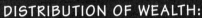

Any accumulation of wealth is to be strictly regulated. First, no citizen is to posess any gold or silver. The city-state's own money will be simple (like Sparta's iron bars), and no citizen may acquire more than four times the natural wealth of his land — any more accumlulation must be placed in common funds. Second, there is to be no poverty, since no citizen will ever be allowed to sink below the wealth of a single plot.

AGAIN, THE REASON FOR THESE LAWS IS THE STA-
BILITY OF THE CITY. AT BOTTOM, THERE IS TO BE NO
DESIRE FOR WEALTH AND ALL IMMODERATE GAIN IS
TO BE FORBIDDEN.

**PLATO BELIEVED THAT IT IS CONCERN FOR
ONE'S OWN WEALTH AND POWER THAT
LEADS PEOPLE AND CITIES INTO CONFLICT.**

BUT UNDER HIS SYSTEM *"GREAT MONEY-MAKING IS
IMPOSSIBLE...THE HYPOTHESIS THAT UNDERLIES
OUR LAWS AIMS AT MAKING THE PEOPLE AS HAPPY
AND FRIENDLY TO ONE ANOTHER AS POSSIBLE."*

THE CLASS STRUCTURE OF THE CITIZENS:

A form of class structure in this less than perfect City is inevitable, since differences will emerge in the accumulation of "private property."

There will be four classes of citizens. This, in turn, will result in different honors and duties for the members of the different classes.

But distinctions among the citizens will never be great — and never wide enough to cause envy and conflict. Within the citizen body, men and women are to be treated equally.

Marriages are to be arranged for the common good of all — **"...in each marriage what must be wooed is not what is most pleasant for one's self, but what is in the interest of the city-state."**

Aside from the citizen body, the city-state will allow resident-foreigners, whose main location will be in the marketplace and whose activities will involve money-making, and slaves, who are considered "property" and who will do most of the menial labor.

THE CITIZENS ARE TO REMAIN AS FREE AS POSSIBLE TO ATTEND TO THE MATTERS OF THE CITY-STATE IN ITS VARIOUS FUNCTIONS AND OFFICES.

THE GOVERNING BODIES:

The governing bodies of the City will consist of a select group of 37 who will act as the Guardians of the Laws, a general Assembly, an elected Council of 360, and a selection of Generals, Priests, and Priestesses, City and Market Regulators and Judges and Juries.

The general thrust of all these guardians and regulators is "to leave nothing unguarded." Everything is to be watched over to make sure that all is in order... and everyone is to be watched over to make sure that each is "minding his own business."

The order and justice that Plato is trying to acheive here will have a high price — the Cretan city-state could be seen as a totalitarian regime.

To produce an entire city-state that is in order and that minds its own business (and hence that is unlike all other Greek city-states that are in constant disorder and at constant war), Plato felt it necessary to mold a city-state (through persuasion and force) into a single body striving for a common good. Since a totalitarian regime *"permits no rival loyalties,"* the only loyalty that the citizen of the Creatan city-state is to have is a loyalty to the common good of all its members:

"...true political art must care not for the private but the common — for the common binds cities together, while the private tears them apart."

"Whoever intends to promulgate laws or cities, and regulate how men should act in regard to public and common actions, but supposes he need not apply a degree of compulsion to private things, supposing each can live his daily life as he wishes, that it's not necessary for everything to be ordered — whoever leaves private things unregulated by law and believes the people will be willing to live with the common and public things regulated by laws — is incorrect in his thinking." (Laws 780a)

"...every man and child insofar as he is able must of necessity become educated, on grounds that they belong more to the City than to those who generated them."

THE NOCTURNAL COUNCIL OF RULERS:

To ensure that the city-state is indeed run for the common good, and to ensure that the laws themselves are truly just, Plato suggests the institution of a secret Nocturnal Council of Rulers.

The Council is to be made up of the ten oldest guardians, along with those who have won honor or virtue, and some younger men of excellence (none under thirty years old). This small group, gathering shortly before dawn, will act as an anchor for the city-state. Its purpose is to make certain that the City and its laws always aim at that which is most excellent and that which contains the true form of virtue. They are to insure that the City always proceeds with a firm and ultimate knowledge of what it is doing.

It seems that this Nocturnal Council is a practical compromise for the philosopher-king. Plato at the end of the dialogue restates his belief that a truly just and virtuous city-state can only come about if its rulers are guided by Reason and are capable of gaining a knowledge of Forms.

PLATO'S LAWS DON'T PAINT A PRETTY PICTURE OF SOCIETY. IN FAIRNESS, THOUGH, GREEK CULTURE DID NOT HAVE THE SENSE OF INDIVIDUALISM THAT WE HAVE TODAY.

SHORTLY AFTER COMPLETING HIS LAST DIALOGUE, PLATO DIED (347 B.C.). AS DIOGENES LAERTIUS REPORTS,

"He died...at a wedding feast, in the first year of the 108th Olympiad, in his eighty-first year.... He was buried in the Academy, where he spent the greatest part of his life in philosophical study.... Phoebus Apollo gave to mortals Asclepius and Plato, the one to save their souls, the other to save their bodies. From a wedding banquet he has passed to that city-state which he founded for himself and planted in the sky."

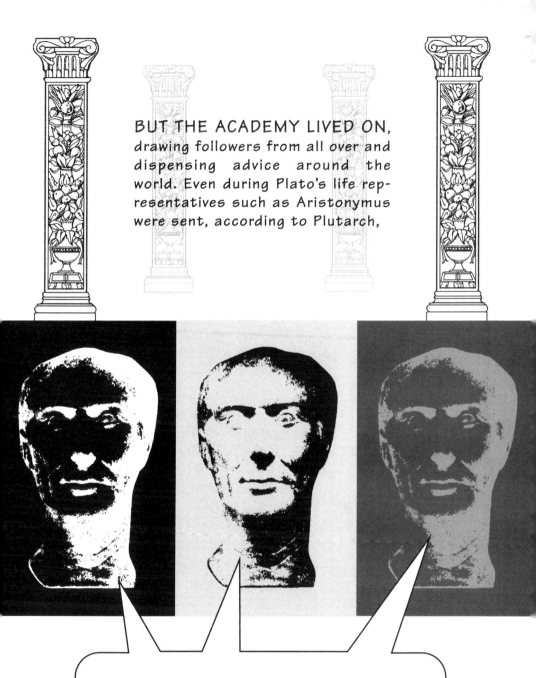

BUT THE ACADEMY LIVED ON, drawing followers from all over and dispensing advice around the world. Even during Plato's life representatives such as Aristonymus were sent, according to Plutarch,

"to the Arcadians to organize the constitution, as was Phormio to Elis and Menedemus to Pyrrha. And Eudoxus drew up laws for Cnidus...."

IT IS AN IRONY OF HISTORY THAT JUST AS PLATO WAS FINISHING HIS THOUGHTS ON THE CITY-STATE, THE REALITY OF THE CITY-STATE WAS COMING TO A CLOSE.

The kingdoms of the far North, under the leadership of Philip of Macedon, were already overwhelming any opposition to their expansion. By the year 338 B.C., most of Greece (Thebes and Athens included) fell under the command of a single force. The endless bickering of the independent city-states was finally brought to a complete close by the unifying conquests of Philip's son, Alexander the Great (353-323 B.C.).

It is also an irony that Plato's brightest student, Aristotle (384-322 B.C.), would soon move beyond his teacher by criticizing the theory of the Forms. In breaking with the Academy, Aristotle declared that we gain nothing by thinking of "the Forms" as some kind of eternal realm above and beyond the objects and actions around us. The Forms, whatever they may be, do not constitute separate reality.

(For a brief period, Aristotle, at Philip's request, became the young Alexander's teacher. He then founded his own school, the Lyceum, and wrote his own works on logic, ethics, metaphysics, and politics.)

Aristotle's
mind looked at
the world
around him.
His work
exhibits a
combination of
observation
and logical
analysis, pre-
sented in dry,
yet powerful,
verse.

Plato's mind
looked ever
upward; his
work is a com-
bination of
mysticism and
rationalism,
embodied in
poetic dis-
course.

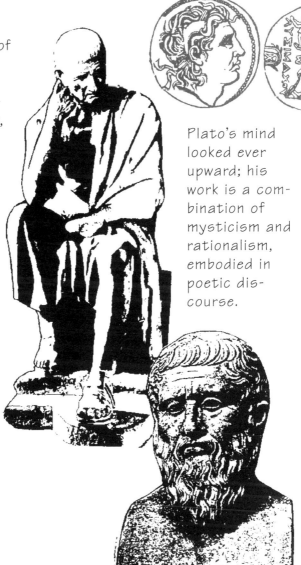

During the silver age of the Roman Empire, Plotinus (204-270 A.D.) created Neo-Platonism, combining Plato's philosophy with a heightened emphasis on God and Salvation. He also dreamed of founding a utopian city called "Platonopolis." His work, the *Enneads*, foreshadowed the great synthesis of Plato and Christianity by St. Augustine (354-430 A.D.).

In Augustine, Plato's division of the world into the Realm of True Being ("Heaven") as well as the separation of the soul from the body (the "immortal soul" distinguished from the "flesh") were given distinctly Christian interpretations. And in dialogues modeled on Plato's, Augustine pursued Plato's ultimate goal — gazing upon the Forms (which Augustine called Summum Bonum and regarded as the Beatific Vision of God).

Only the *Timaeus* was available in Latin translation during the Middle Ages, and it became one of the most widely read books of that time (good for advice to astrologers, who were quite in vogue back then). Around the middle of the 13th century, however, the works of Aristotle became available in Latin and were "Christianized" by St. Thomas Aquinas (1225-1274). The writings of Plato's student thus came, for a time, to overshadow those of the teacher himself.

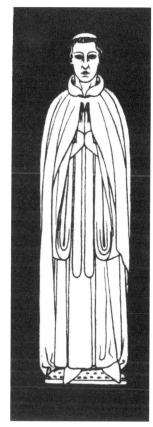

During the Renaissance, Western Europe rediscovered classical Greek thought and literature. A new "humanism" replaced the dry scholasticism of the universities — and Plato's writings were all the rage among the new intellectuals. In fact, Cosimo de'Medici founded the Florence Academy in imitation of Plato's famous school.

It was at this time that the phrase "Platonic love" was coined. In The Book of the Courtier (1571), Baldessare Castiglione writes: "If the gentleman shall be pert...she will give him such answer that he may clearly understand he is causing her annoyance...I would have her yield to her lover nothing but her spirit."

Plato's influence is found in the debates between the Rationalists (Descartes, Leibniz, Spinoza) and the Empiricists (Locke, Berkeley, Hume). In 1781, Immanuel Kant tried to reconcile these views in his Critique of Pure Reason. To the Rationalists he said: "Thoughts without content are empty." To the Empiricists he said: "Intuitions without concepts are blind."

With the rise and spread of Fascism across Europe in the 1930s, some saw the totalitarian politics of Plato coming to fruition. "Plato was led along a path on which he compromised his integrity with every step he took.... He was forced to combat free thought...In spite of his own hatred of tyranny...he was led to defend the most tyrannical measures." (Karl Popper, The Open Society and Its Enemies)

The same problems may be seen in the bureaucratic communism established by Lenin and Mao. And today the battle rages on, with neither Plato's utopian communism nor modern proletarian communism able to supply the people with enough freedom, food, and VCRs...

EPILOGUE

Plato's questions remain as real for us today as they were 2500 years ago...and as human beings, we cannot avoid their presence nor shirk our responsibility to attempt to answer them:What is Justice?

What is Truth?

What is Beauty?

What kind of Society should we build?

How do we know what we know?

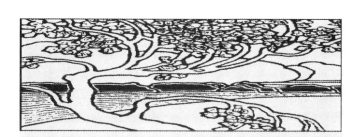

INDEX